# Black Folx Alchemy

Belongs to:

ISBN: 979-8-218-20934-6

To my mother Jackie,

from where I received an inheritance of faith
an abundance of magic, and a sense of humor.
I am here because of your fervent prayers.
The Bible says of a virtuous woman: "Her
children will call her blessed".
Well, we all call you blessed.
Thank you for the gift of your presence, your
wisdom, your laugh. The world is better
because of you.

# Introduction

**Black Folx are magical. Look anywhere across the Diaspora, and you will see abundant evidence of African-descendent people being magical wonders. The ways in which we alchemize the world around us** is masterful: for centuries, we have taken the traumas of our experience and transmute it into beauty, into rhythm, into a more lovely and just world. Yet, there are so few resources that center Black folx and Diasporic African practices at the core of spirituality —especially in the world of manifestation. Within our own cultural communities, we have a wealth of knowledge and practices about everything from herbal healing to energy transmutation. We are our own gurus and we deserve to be recognized for the magic that we are.

**We have transformed whole cultures like Marsha P. Johnson at Stonewall; wrote words so powerful they shake nations like James Baldwin. Made freedom out of oppression like Queen Nanny of the Maroons in Jamaica; used our powers to spark revolutions like Cecile Fatiman in Haiti.**

All across the African Diaspora are folx who have mastered all the principles of magic, manifestation, and alchemy and used it for the collective good. Many of our own mothers and grandmothers often had to make a dollar out of 15 cents, make enough out of not enough, make a way out of no way—armed with a few herbs, a song, a dance, a prayer, a proverb, or a laying on of hands. If that ain't magic, I don't know what is.

*It is apart of our cultural inheritance to call forth heaven when it's hell on Earth.*

We come from Wise Elders and Praying Folx, Iyanifas and Manbos, Curanderas and Espiritistas, Hoodoos and Herbalists, Preachers, Teachers, and Evangelists. Yet, the mainstream spirituality industry is absent of the wisdoms of Black women across time. The "spiritual masters" of our day are overwhelming male, and—if they are women—are overwhelmingly white.

Racism and misogynoir, homophobia and transphobia would have us believe that our own cultural models and examples are not enough, but this is deception. We have built and destroyed worlds, time and time again. Much of the current world that exists owes it's very existence to Black folx who, time and time again, choose to create freer worlds for all to live.

This workbook is a love letter to us, a witnessing of our magic and a commitment to hold the light. We know the way forward. For ourselves, for our communities, and for the world.

So to all us beautiful Black folx—across all spectrums of our community—we are more than enough. We are divine light made manifest, and we deserve all the joy, hope, and healing we can hold. Create the reality that deserves you. Call forth all your good.

Love,

Candice

# How To Use This Workbook

This workbook is written with the idea of rest in mind. As you complete, remember that rest is a necessary part of any spiritual or emotional process.

The workbook is designed to build on top of itself, starting with "Shadow Work" and culminating with "Sowing Seeds: Community Care". Each section integrates another aspect of wisdom and exploration that can be used to aid you in developing the rituals and practices that are most beneficial to you and your community. There are also pages that encourage you to document what arises during meditation and deep listening sessions.

Included in the back of the book are a Dream Journal and a Miracle Tracker. Tracking your dreams is an important part of shadow work as well as spiritual practices as it is a profound place for symbolism and messages from guides, our inner knowing and higher self, or from ancestors. Also, as you become clearer on what good you are calling in to your life, it will become important to document the miracles that occur on your path. Miracles are everywhere and happening all ways! Align yourself with the flow of miracles by growing your perception of them.

All of the practices are inspired by many different African and African Diasporic practices, cosmologies, and spiritual modalities,. The activities chosen have as an intention to honor that wisdom which is open to us all while keeping sacred those practices which require initiation and/or spiritual tutelage to handle.

**ABOUT RITUALS**

Each section of this workbook has an exercise that guides you to create a ritual for yourself. Rituals, as used here, are any activity or process done with the intent to transform. Rituals are made sacred by our own reverence and as such, are to be handled with care and mindfulness. In African and Diasporic traditions, rituals are communal, healing, and typically involve dancing and rhythm. In creating your rituals, work with the spirits and the energies that you know. Examples include personal beloved ancestors, the energy of divine, unconditional love, the spirit of joy, etc. I do not recommend calling in or invoking specific spirits, orishas, or lwas unless you are an initiate of such practices or under the spiritual tutelage of an Initiate who can guide you in best practices. Remember, that each ritual involves an opening to begin the work and a closing to finish the work. Offering thanks and gratitude are an amazing way to energetically close a ritual.

## ABOUT ANCESTRAL ALTARS

There is a section that involves connecting to the wisdom of our ancestors, whether personal ancestors or our collective ancestors. If you are interested in having a dedicated space within your home to build relationship and connection with your ancestors, an altar space may be great for you. Working with your own ancestors does not need any initiation into a particular spiritual practice; ancestor altars are common in cultures all across the world and they have similar things in common. For an altar, you may place a cloth or covering on a clean space or tabletop. Some customs the color is white, for others it is red. Choose what most aligns with your ancestors. A candle (red or white) is placed, as well as incense. You may offer fruit or food items that your ancestors liked, including alcohol. A glass of water is also common, as well as a plant. Pictures of your ancestors as well as their names are places, but do not place pictures that include living people. This is a gathering space and feel free to add items that resonate with you. Fresh flowers, crystals—whatever honors the space in loving connection. Talk to your ancestors there. You may choose to begin conversation by ringing a bell, tapping a stick, or using a Tibetan singing bowl. Tell them about your day, write your petitions (be specific and include deadlines), offer gratitude, and just spend time in communion.

Remember, this is about your and your ancestors. As the relationship grows, they will show you what they want on the altar and you will learn new ways to communicate to them. Enjoy the evolving connection and let love guide you.

# Shadow Work

Shadow work is a term used in psychology and personal development to describe the process of exploring and integrating the unconscious parts of one's personality, also known as the "shadow." This refers to the aspects of ourselves that we repress, deny, or disown due to societal, cultural, or personal beliefs and values, but which still influence our behavior and emotions. The aim of shadow work is to increase self-awareness, heal past traumas, and integrate the shadow into one's overall sense of self, leading to personal growth and increased emotional intelligence. This can be done through a variety of methods, including journaling, therapy, meditation, and dream work.

Shadow work that doesn't consider how capitalism, colonialism, racism, enslavement, gendered violence, homophobia, transphobia, and poverty affect our spiritual and personal development is grossly incomplete. I would dare say that for Black Folx, the shadow work is understanding the ways we have internalized the darkness of a society that devalues our lives. The shadow is how we limit our lives by internalizing ideas that our worth is determined by how much money or capital we have, how large or small our bodies are, the color of our skin and the length and texture of our hair, our minds and bodies function "normally," how well we fit into the idea of what a "man" or "woman" *should* be: how they should look, dress, or act to be considered worthy of love and respect.

This shadow is often passed around between us, projected on us or we project it on each other.

To come into power, is to step out from the shadows of this society and stand in the light of our ability to regenerate. We were born worthy. We have nothing else to prove.

# "WHERE THE WOUND IS, IS ALSO WHERE THE GIFT IS."

*A Dagara Proverb,*
*Burkina Faso, West Africa*

**What pieces of your identity are connected to a painful story? Are you able to forgive and release those pieces?**

# I CAN TELL A NEW STORY.

Color the affirmation.

# I am grateful for ...

# “SPEAK THE TRUTH AND SHAME THE DEVIL.”

*An African American Proverb*

A guided writing musical meditation is available for this journal prompt at https://alchemistplayground.gumroad.com

Use code ALCHEMIST for free access.

**What are the tyrannies you swallow day by day and attempt to make your own, until you will sicken and die of them, still in silence?**

**-Audre Lorde**

# I am releasing...

**What wounds are you now able to reclassify as a gift?**

# Ritual

[ intention + ceremony ]

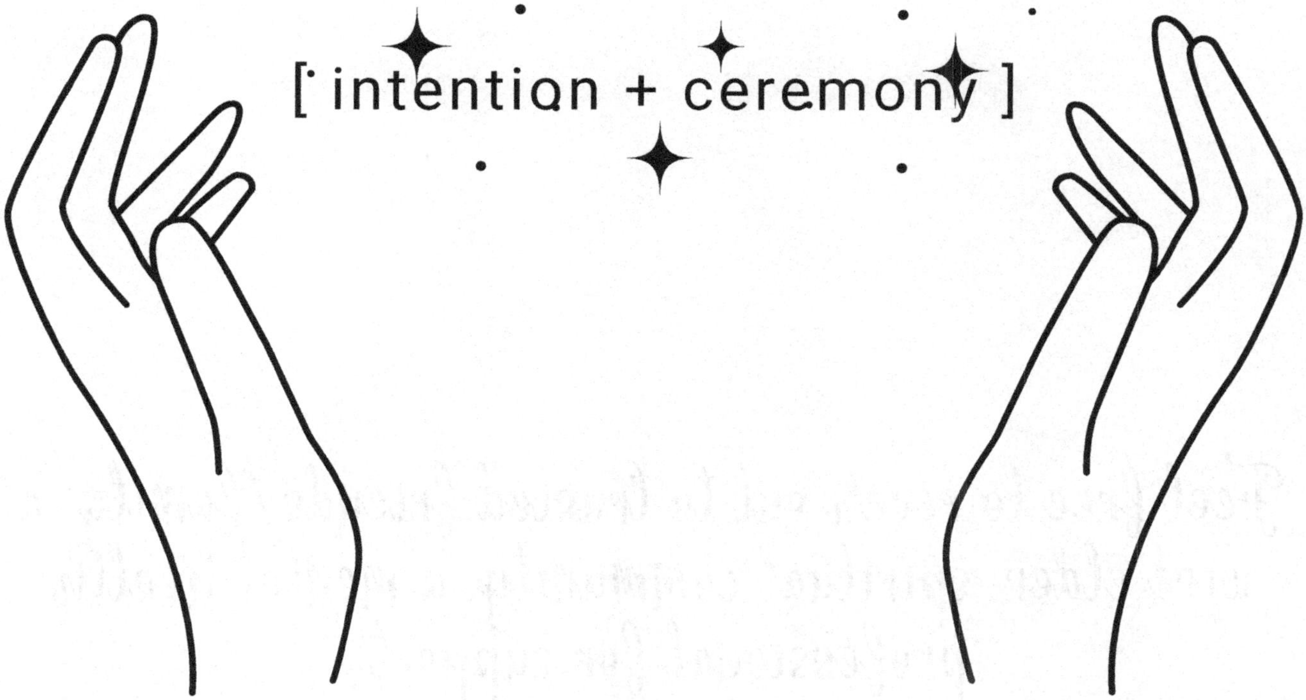

Grief & Loss are natural parts of the cycle of life, but are often unspoken of.

Create a grief ritual to honor the sacredness of your grief and to recognize your ability to grow larger than your grief.

Feel free to reach out to trusted friends/family, a wise elder, spiritual community, a mental health professional for support.

# I am calling forth...

And so it is.
Ase.
Amen.

And so it is.
Ase.
Amen.

# LIFE IS HAPPENING THROUGH ME, NOT TO ME.

Color the affirmation.

Set a timer for 5 minutes.
Close your eyes and place your hands on a part of your body that needs an infusion of loving energy.
Imagine yourself well—full of vibrant energy, and radiating dazzling light.
Feel this light all around you, enveloping you in a loving embrace.

Breathe that in.

# Meditation & Deep Listening

# Ancestors

Across the Diaspora, It is customary for us to honor the cultural/spiritual/political ancestors that positively shaped our societies; to remember our beloved family members with stories at family gatherings; or to pour libation during ceremonies.

*Ancestors are the shoulders upon whom we stand. We often say today that we are our ancestors' wildest dreams.*

We find in their lives an example of how to live (and sometimes how not to live) and there is a wisdom from lived experience that is made available to us through oral stories, through books, through dreams, or through divination.

Whatever your spiritual background or comfort level, there are ways to honor our ancestors:

*Research your ancestry: Start by learning about your family history, including the names and stories of your ancestors. This will help you to connect with them on a personal level.

*Create an ancestral altar: Set up an altar in your home or a special place where you can honor your ancestors. You can include pictures, symbols, and objects that are meaningful to you and your ancestors.

*Offer food and drink: Ancestral veneration practices often involve offering food and drink to the ancestors. We may pour libation ( liquid or alcohol onto the ground) as a way of honoring them. This is a way to provide sustenance and show appreciation for their presence in your life.

*Light candles or incense: Lighting candles or incense is a way to symbolize the presence of ancestors and to create a peaceful and spiritual atmosphere.

*Pray or meditate: Spend time in quiet reflection, meditation, or prayer to connect with your ancestors and to offer thanks and respect.

*Keep a journal: Keeping a journal is a way to document your ancestral veneration practices, to reflect on your experiences, and to deepen your connection to your ancestors.

*Celebrate special occasions: Many cultures have special holidays or rituals that are dedicated to honoring ancestors, like Dia De Los Muertos in Mexico or Fét Gede in Haiti. It may also occur at family gatherings or on a beloved ancestors birthday. Whatever it is, make sure to celebrate these occasions in a meaningful way.

**What ancestors, whether by lineage or by culture, do I feel strong kinship with? What aspects of them am I proud to embody ? What aspects of theirs would I like to embody more of?**

# Meditation & Deep Listening

# I HAVE A RICH INHERITANCE OF WISDOM INSIDE ME.

Color the affirmation.

**What are the ways I am connecting to ancestral wisdoms? How might I strengthen those connections?**

# Ritual

[ intention + ceremony ]

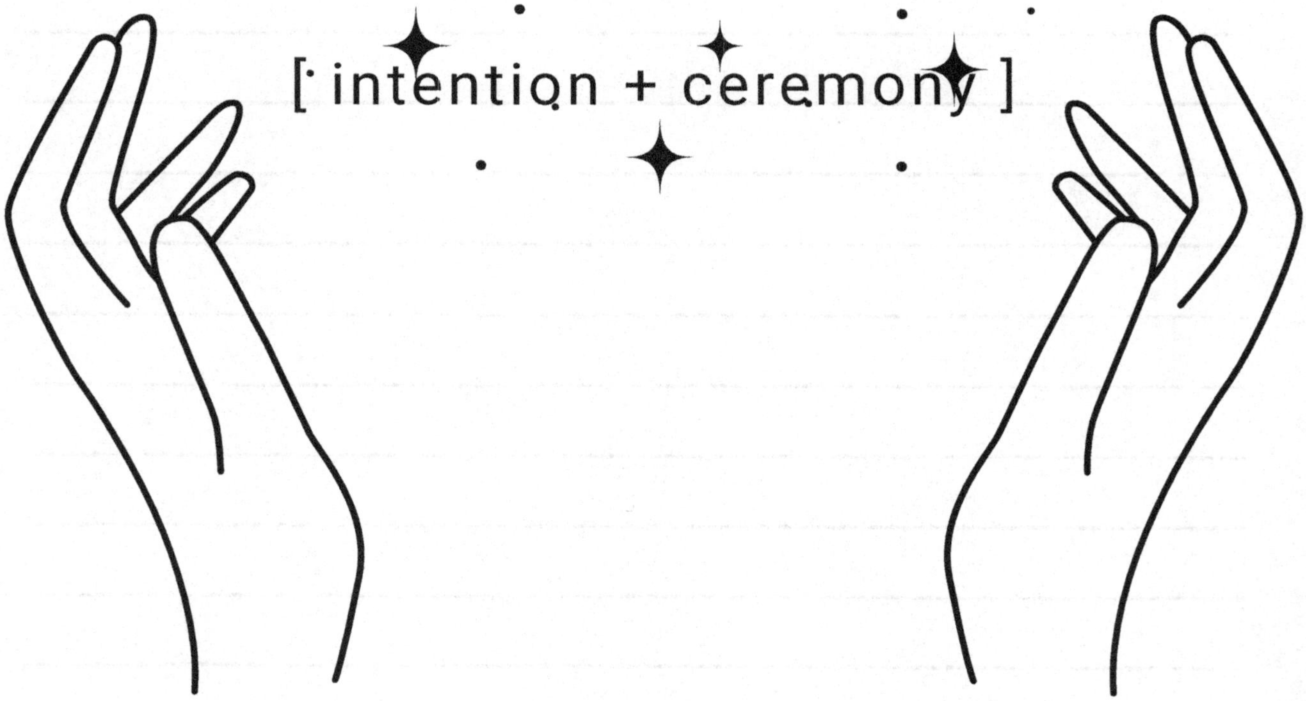

Create a ritual to honor the ancestral wisdom within you.

Pour libation for them as you speak the names of the ancestors that are important to you.

As you honor them, ask for their support to help you honor your role as a future ancestor.

**As a future ancestor, what can I do in this present moment to leave a positive legacy for those who come after me?**

As a future ancestor, what can I do in this present moment to leave a positive legacy for those who come after me?

# I am grateful for ...

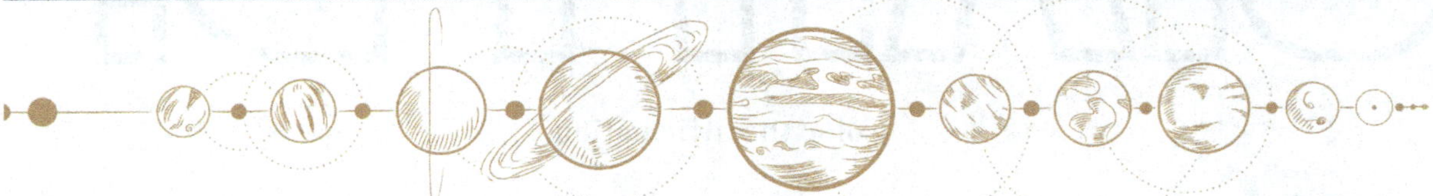

# I STAND ON THE BACKS OF GIANTS.

Color the affirmation.

# I am releasing...

# I am calling forth...

And so it is.
Ase.
Amen.

And so it is.
Ase.
Amen.

# Working With The Elements

"THE TREES, THE ROCKS, THE BIRDS... THOSE ARE PART OF THE POOL OF ANCESTORS THAT WE CAN ALL WORK WITH."

*Subonfu Somè, Dagara Elder*

A guided writing meditation called "Writing As Ancestral Connection" is available at https://alchemistplayground.gumroad.com Use code: ALCHEMIST for free access.

The next few pages are for notetaking.

# Introduction to Dagara Elements

The Dagara people are an ethnic group that lives in Burkina Faso and Ghana of West Africa. In the Dagara's cosmology, the community or village is made up of humans, the elements, and the spiritual world which includes ancestors and a host of other entities and spirits. Elders Malidoma Patrice Somè and Subonfu Somè through their books, workshops, and teachings brought the wisdom of the Dagara people to those of us in the West to draw upon. For many of us with ancestry traced to that region of West Africa, we may find some innate kinship with their worldview.

For the Dagara, there are 5 elements, and each person is born into a clan that corresponds to one of these elements. Determined by the last digit of your birth year, your elemental clan offers guidance on how you may contribute to the village and the complete balance and harmony of the humans with each other, the humans with nature, as well as with the spirit realm.

Although we each are born into a specific clan, it is important to embody the other elements as all the elements together support our unique fingerprint and mission in the world.
To learn more, read the works of Dagara elders and spiritual teachers Dr. Malidoma Patrice Somè and Subonfu Somè.

The five elements are:

**Fire**, the original element of origin, is the doorway to the ancestors and the Spirit World. It represents our own spirits and fuels our capacity to act. Fire clan people are in touch with spirits and ancestors; they feel themselves straddling the physical and spiritual worlds. They may not fit in so neatly with society because of this. Fire clan people may need to remember that a fire out or control will burn a village, but a calm fire warms a community. *Birth years ending in 2 or 7 (For example, 1982 and 1997 are fire clan.) Color: red*

**Water** is seen as the doorways to the Otherworld. Water represents cleansing, reconciliation, purification and peace-making. Water also connects to grief and the tears needed to cleanse the soul. Water clan people are slow to anger and able to peacefully settle disputes in the village. An out of balance water clan person may live in denial and become conflict avoidant instead of conflict resolving. *Birth years ending in 1 or 6 (For example, 1976 or 2001). Color: blue*

**Earth** is the element of home, comfort, grounding, unconditional love. Earth clan are at home wherever they are and are natural nurturers—with a heart for creating and sustaining community. An earth clan person who is not embodying their element may feel ungrounded, unloved, or become a resentful martyr—giving too much. A community with balanced earth clan people will be welcoming to others, inclusive, and loving. *Birth years ending in 0 and 5 (For example, 1985 and 1960). Color: yellow*

**Mineral** is the elemental energy of creativity, memory, communication and story keeping. Mineral is embodied by bones (think the wisdom in your bones), rocks, stones, gems and crystals. These are seen to carry within them the memory of earth or memory of our origins, society, and purpose. Mineral clan people are born carrying wisdom and memory, and are drawn to stories, symbols, and mythology of cultures. They may become artist, actors, poets. Out of balance, their penchant for communication may turn to argumentation. *Birth years ending in 4 and 9 (For example, 1984 and 1999). Color: white*

**Nature** is the element that represents change, transformation, flexibility, life, death, and magic. Nature is all the animals, plants and natural landscapes,. This elements recognizes that all elements of nature have a consciousness and can transmit messages between the physical and other world. Just as nature is ever changing, the nature clan person has a keen ability to transform and change forms and considered natural magicians. They are authentic and encourage others to be authentic, embody their magic, and have fun again. A nature clan person may need to be careful not to use their magic harm others. *Birth years ending in 3 and 8 (For example 1963 and 1998). Color: green*

*Refernce Material: The Healing Wisdom of Africa by Malidoma Patrice Somé, published 1999*

# I AM AT HOME EVERY-WHERE I AM.

Color the affirmation.

**Which element did you feel most connected to? In what ways can you integrate the wisdom from this element?**

Take time to sit quietly in nature. No music, no phone, no distractions.

Sit with your back against a tree that you feel drawn to.

Open your heart. Listen with more than your ears, and see with more than your eyes.

**What wisdom does nature have for you? What healing is available to me you as a gift from the nature around you?**

Align with the medicine of mineral element by calling forth a power stone.

As you move about your days, utilize your inner knowing to follow your intuition towards a particular rock, gemstone, or mineral that resonates with your energy.

If you find it in nature, be sure to make an offering or exchange in gratitude for it.

When you receive it, spend time holding your stone to discern its properties and power for you.

Write about your reflections, experience, and any messages received.

Create a healing bath to release a painful story you carry.

Speak to the water your intentions and desires.

When you get into the bath, meditate on your desire. Feel the water‘s assistance in helping wash away the residue of bitterness, regret, resentment.

Invoke the water‘s ability to flow in service of helping you forgive and release yourself and anyone else as necessary.

Repeat as often as necessary. Ask for spiritual assistance.

Write about your experience.

# I am grateful for ...

Use the next page to write petitions to your ancestors for assistance.

Take time to meditate for clarity regarding the areas you need ancestral assistance.

Write what you want to task them with. Be specific. Put relevant amounts and deadlines.

When complete, rip this page out and offer it to the element of fire.

As it burns, thank the ancestors and spiritual helpers and guides for their assistance.

Give the ashes to the earth.

(Use caution and safe practices while working with fire.)

# I am releasing...

# I AM MADE OF THE SAME ELEMENTS AS THE STARS.

Color the affirmation.

# I am calling forth...

And so it is.
Ase.
Amen.

*And so it is.*
*Ase.*
*Amen.*

# Meditation & Deep Listening

# Building Worlds

World Building is a phrase often used in the science fiction and fantasy writing genres to describe the ways in which an author will use their imagination to paint a picture of a world so vivid that readers can see it for themselves and feel themselves within it.

Black science fiction writers offer us examples of how to create a world so lush and rich in the imagination, that we can begin to bring that world into physical reality. In Hermeneutics, it's called "As Above, So Below". From the immaterial realm come the ideas, and then—through a birthing process of sorts—the idea is pushed into the physical realm. It becomes tangible.

Black artists are activists of the imagination. N.K. Jemisin and Octavia Butler are two prolific Black science fiction writers that show us that we are only limited by the limits of our own imaginations. If you can see it, it can become real. They tell stories of brown skinned female protagonists who save the world through their intellect and know how, through their skills and supernatural abilities. They tell of women, like us, who create and destroy worlds. We can do the same.

Consider Harriet Tubman: while enslaved, Harriet (then named Araminta Ross) has a vision of Black people free. However, her current reality did not match that vision. Holding that vision tightly against her heart, she became instrumental in bringing that reality forth, not just for herself but for some of her own contemporaries and for so many of us who have come behind her. That reality existed only in vision, but became tangible. The world we live in, the freedoms we have access to was built by the audacious imaginations of Black women who came before us.

The current reality is the starting point, not the determining factor. The current reality is in flux and is within the power of your imagination to change.
Art and Imagination are tools to build another world right on top of the one that exists.

It equires only audacity. You are already powerful enough. Powerfully create your own world.

**What does a world where you are free, supported, abundantly resourced and loved look like? Feel like? Sound like?**

# “IF YOU BAWN FI HENG, YU CYAA DROWN”

*A Jamaican Proverb meaning”your destiny will be fulfilled”.*

# WHEN I CHANGE MY MIND, I CHANGE THE WORLD.

Color the affirmation.

Roleplay: Spend 5 minutes actively living in your desired reality.

Talk to yourself in a mirror as your desired self.

Imagine your environment as you wish it to be and interact with it.

Have conversations that you desire to have.

Write a fantasy or science fiction retelling of your life story. Imagine your future. What magical elements will benefit you as protagonist of your story?

# Meditation & Deep Listening

"IF YOU DON'T KNOW WHO YOU ARE, ANYONE CAN NAME YOU.

IF ANYONE CAN NAME YOU, YOU WILL ANSWER TO ANYTHING."

*An African Proverb.*

# Ritual

[ intention + ceremony ]

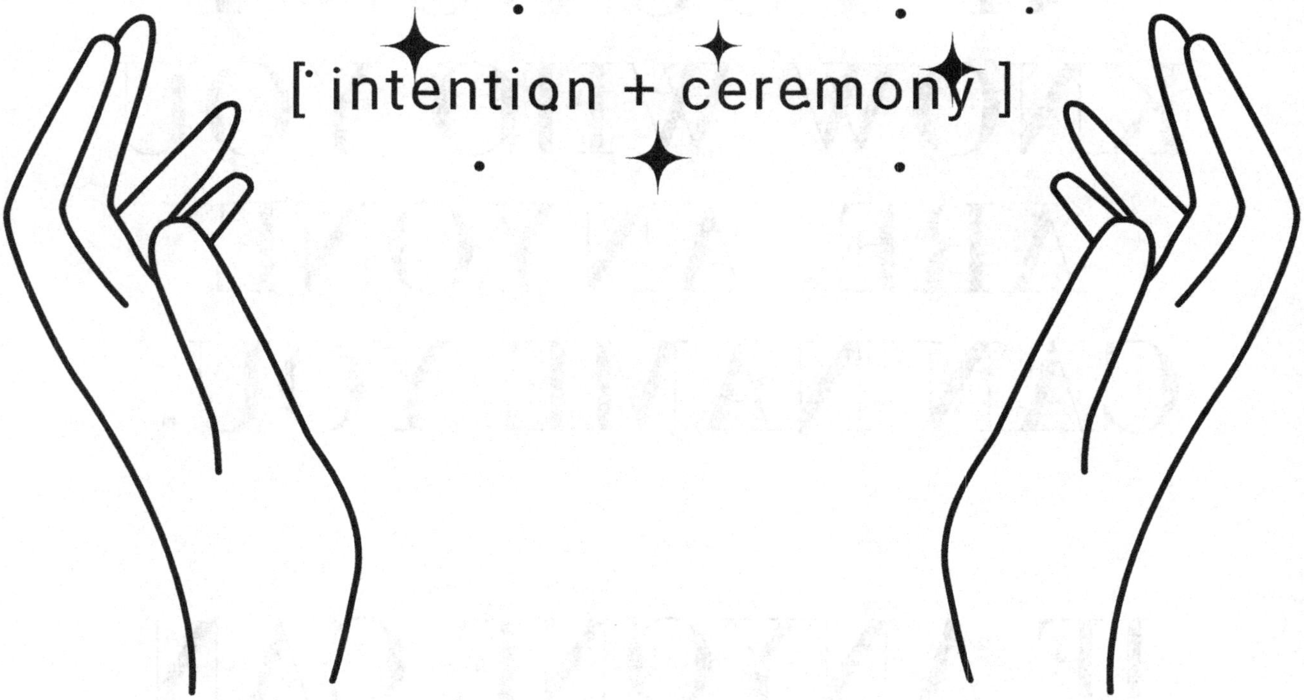

Create a naming ceremony to give yourself a new name.

Choose a name or title that represents your divinity and destiny.

At your naming ceremony, make peace with the names  or titles you are choosing to leave behind.

**My new name is:**
**I am grateful for...**

# I am grateful for...

# AS I BELIEVE IT TO BE, AND SO IT IS.

Color the affirmation.

# I am releasing...

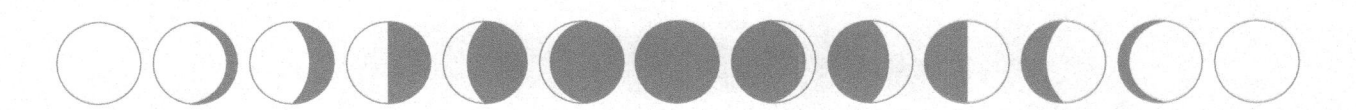

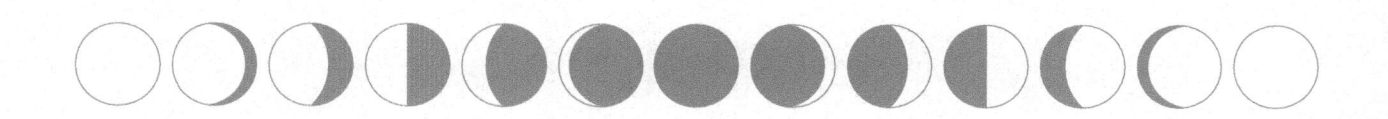

# I am calling forth...

And so it is.
Ase.
Amen.

And so it is.
Ase.
Amen.

# Manifesting Miracles

# Manifesting Miracles

The Law of Attraction and Manifesting have taken up a lot of space in the mainstream spiritual discourse, and for good reason. All of us want to know the keys to gaining access to necessary resources and capital to sustain our lifestyles and support our families.

However, the most prominent thought leaders of those practices often don't look like us. The strategies they provide rely heavily on unspoken Western European cultural contexts. One example is the ways in which their strategies rely heavily on the mind and affirmations but fail to integrate the body in the manifestation process. Black folks always use our bodies when we invoke spirit! Another example is the emphasis on quiet, solo experiences of manifestation (quiet affirmations) which is rooted in Western European emphasis on individuality and the notion of decorum. Their spiritual practices take the cultural value of emotional reservation, which exists in stark contrast to Black cultural understandings of spirit as communal, expressive, and—loud.

*Even more concerning, many of the foremost practitioners have no critical understanding of race and capitalism in their teachings.*

We do not need to look far to find manifestation gurus in our own lineages. The practices look and sound much different, but the metaphysics behind it is similar. I would say we manifest—with more flavor.

It looked like a Holy Ghost dance or Vodou trance. It may have been your mother washing the floor with holy water or black eyed peas and greens for the new year. It may have looked like blowing cinnamon into the front door or a laying on of hands in the church. It was a prayer line; a divination and ebo. It was intercession prayer or placing food on an ancestral altar. These practices are ours and they work! We do not need to reinvent the wheel; we just need to appreciate the wealth of knowledge that has already been left for us in our DNA.

Whatever the spiritual system or practices of your family or ancestor, we KNOW how to call forth our good, with our words, our bodies, and our hearts.

So what are the basic steps of manifesting, or as a Black church mother might say "calling heaven forth"?

*The steps are:*

*Make a clear request/set a clear intention.*

*Practice Gratitude.*

*Surrender control.*

*Take Inspired Action.*

*Receive.*

**Let's explore what strategies the African Diaspora has to offer us to manifest our desires for a magical life.**

You may have heard the word "Àse being spoken after a prayer or as an affirmation of agreement. It is a word that is used in Yoruba based spiritual practices (and also taught by Dagara elder and shaman Dr. Malidoma Somè of Burkina Faso.) Àse is often understood to mean "and so it is", and represents the power to speak something into being.

Many teachers from outside our cultural contexts emphasize practices that are individual, quiet, and intellectual. However, many of our cultural practices are communal, vocal, and movement based. We combine powerful affirmations in song with dance; and we often do this in communal settings.

This may have looked like the holy shouts in Black churches where congregants danced and shouted to God with hands raised calling for a miracle.
It may have looked like walking in circles in a specific place and repeating psalms.
It looked like being 7 years old and watching my Christian mother stand at the open back door and rebuke and bind the spirit of poverty from our home (and today she owns multiple properties).

It looks like a ring shout in the US South.
It looks like an entire village singing songs and walking in a circle calling for rain during planting season.
It looks like a Dagara ancestor ritual where petitions where the entire community uses strong emotion (and even strong knowledge) to command the ancestors to positively intervene in affairs of importance.
It is a yell, a moan, a song and dance over drums during rituals across the Caribbean. It is an intercessory prayer to Jesus and laying on of hands.
It is loudly beseeching the ancestors to assist in making a way.
It is St. John's root and cinnamon with powerful commands.

And when we have poured the libations, cried the tears, made the requests known—there is the offering: the action taken in expectancy as a show of gratitude for miracle that is on its way. My Mother would instruct me that after I had prayed about my issue, to do the "happy dance"; a dance of victory because God bears and the battle has already been won. This may look like a food offering at the ancestral altar or at the ocean or a river. It may be an offering of praise and "Thank you God". But it is understood: **offer gratitude and reciprocal action.**

And then, it's time to listen for the revelation and stay open to the signs. This may come in a dream, a prophetic word during a phone call, a divination. For Black Folx, the process of manifestation and creation is not a rote series of steps, but a constant dance with the divine.

It has always been our way of life to create with our entire beings.

So many of our cultural practices, whether it is the ways we practice Christianity, or it is through Vodou, Hoodoo, Ifa, Cantomblè, Lucumi, or Santeria, have been viewed through a Western lens that considers our ways of being less than.

Yet the magic of our folx was more than enough to see them through the darkest of times. We can keep what works while adding to our own arsenal, but let us never forget that we come to the table already enough.

Your process can look as unique as you do, and use whatever traditions and methods work best for you and feel most aligned with you.

“ASK GOD, THEN DANCE IT IN. PRAISE BRINGS GOD’S ATTENTION”

*Elder Wisdom from my Mother, Jackie D’Meza, LMFT*

Ask a Wise Elder in your family or spiritual community for their wisdom on how to bring a miracle forth.

Write down what they say and reflect upon it.

Use the next page to draw yourself as a "Magic Maker of Miracles".
Use colors that bring you joy.

Write the next journal prompt from the perspective of your desired reality.

Today, I am grateful for ...

# "SA KI PA TOUYE OU, LI ANGRESE OU"

*A Haitian Proverb meaning "what doesn't kill you, fattens you." If you endure, you will be stronger.*

# MIRACLES ARE MY NATURAL WAY OF LIFE.

Color the affirmation.

**How might my current life look different if I truly believed that the game of life is rigged in my favor. What might I change about my career, home, family life, love life, my self?**

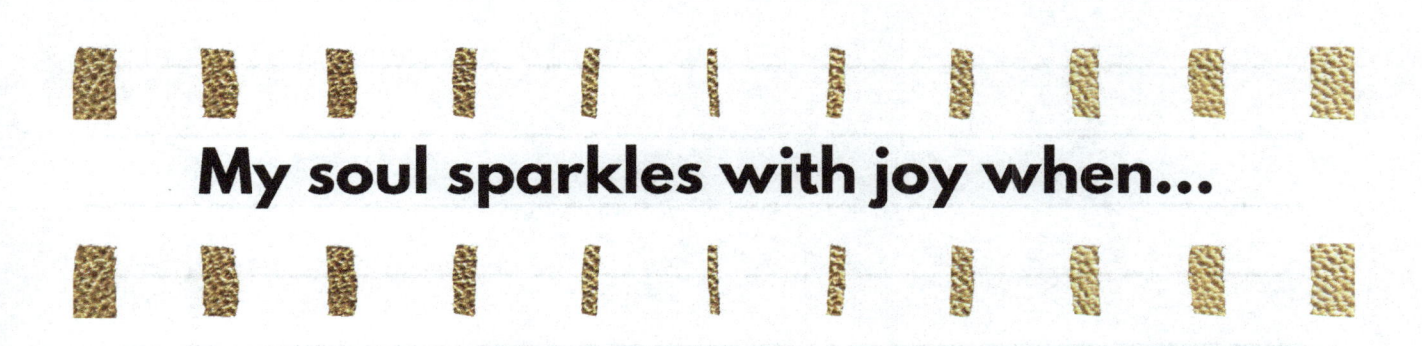

**My soul sparkles with joy when...**

# I am releasing...

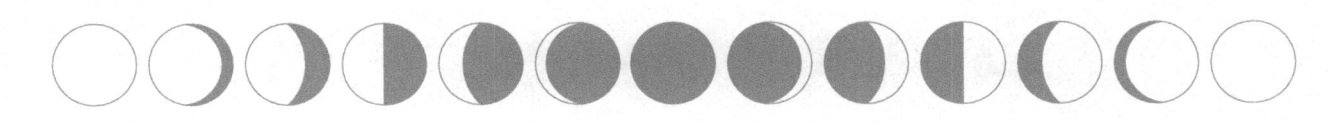

With the power of your Àse (the creative and authoritative power of your spoken word), Bind the negative spirits from around you, your home, your business, and your loved ones.

Bind:
Poverty
Abuse
Bitterness & Fury
Discord
(Add your own)

You may choose to combine with the recitation of verses or psalms, ringing bells, walking around your home as you speak, singing spiritual songs, laying on off hands or herbal work. Choose the activity that most aligns with your spiritual traditions and/or the spiritual traditions of your ancestors.

# I AM THE MIRACLE.

Color the affirmation.

# I am calling forth...

And so it is.
Ase.
Amen.

And so it is.
Ase.
Amen.

# Ritual

[ intention + ceremony ]

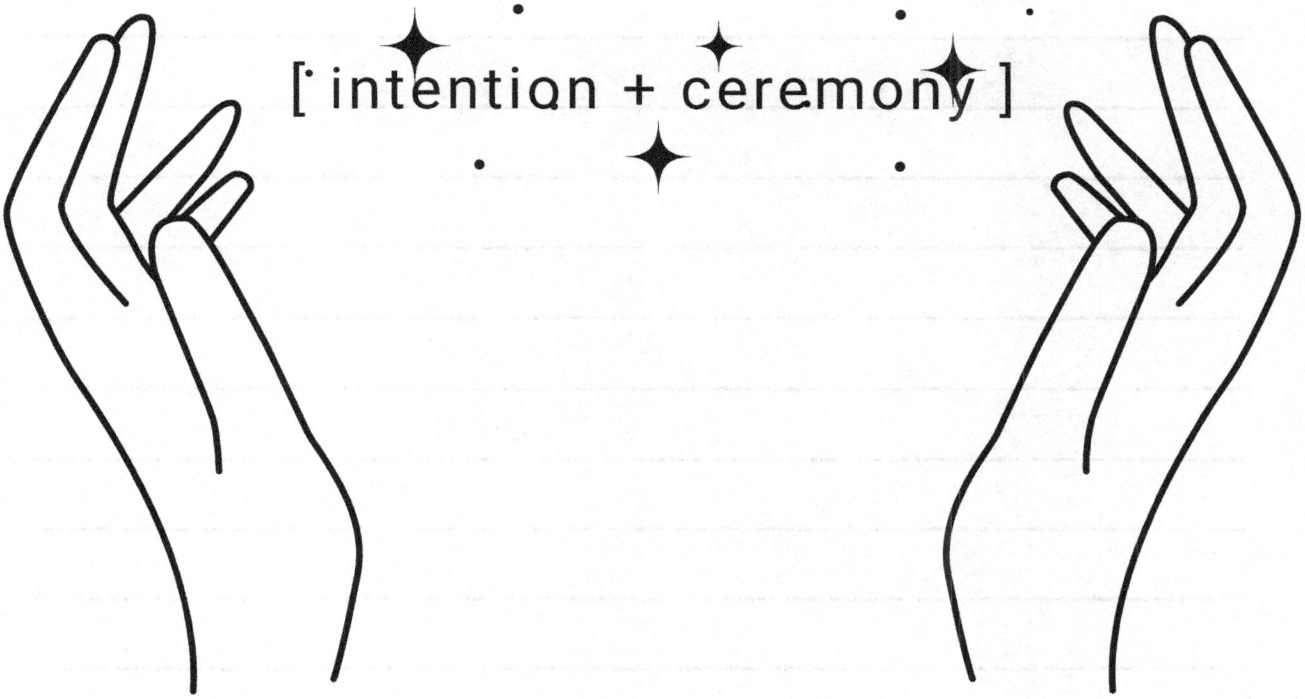

Create a ritual to call forth your good.
Be specific.

Be creative: use song, dance, chants, shouts, and any natural elements that call to you.

You may choose to invoke wise and loving ancestors and tell them in detail how to support you.

# Sowing Seeds

COMMUNITY CARE

"I am because we are" is an African adage that has undergirded our spiritual practices across the Diaspora. It is so easy for Western-based practices to have an overemphasis on individual achievement as the entire basis for manifesting. To fall into this worldview would be detrimental to us Black Folx. Our individual safety and wellness can empower us to create safety and wellness for others; ensuring our basic needs (and even our luxurious wants) are met is an important step in the spiritual process but it is merely one step. The next step is to ask ourselves: how may I be of service? How can I bring more good into the world, for my family, for my friends, and or the community and world at large.

Elders Malidoma Somè and Subonfu Somè share much about the Dagara people's expansive views of community: community is about our connections with each other, our connections to the natural world around us, and connections to the spirit world and the ancestors. To have a healthy community is to create harmonious relationships between humans, the earth, and the spirit. That is the village. There is an interdependence between all three of these elements that is critical to our survival on the planet and an alchemical practice focused on activating our interconnectedness is important to our collective wellness and individual health.

Alchemy harnesses the interrelationships between the visible and invisible worlds, and we can't forget that the earth itself is apart of our village and spiritual practice. Ensuring that our ways of being in the world nurture the very Earth that is housing and nurturing us is critical in this time. Becoming involved in practices that preserve resources, regenerate the Earth and reduce the exploitation of its resources is a major part of our liberation. We must begin to care for all the parts of our village: sowing seeds so that our future generations can harvest the fruit of our labors now.

# "MEN ANPIL CHAY PA LOU."

*A Haitian Proverb meaning"many hands lighten the load".*

**What is your definition of "community"? Who is in your community? How have you determined who is included and who is excluded?**

**In what ways do I use my magic and divinity to create joy and good for others? Are there spaces in which I can be more active in creating more love in my connections with others?**

Provide something of tangible benefit to someone within your community.

Examples include:

a meal/setting up a meal train for a caretaker/new parent

a donation to a mutual aid organization in your area

volunteering time for a community organization, or an elderly person

a financial gift to someone, anonymously if possible.

Invoke the law of return. As you provide for others, you will be provided for.

# WE ARE EACH OTHER'S KEEPER.

Color the affirmation.

# "HAND GO, HAND COME."

*A Ghanaian Proverb meaning"the way you give is the way you receive".*

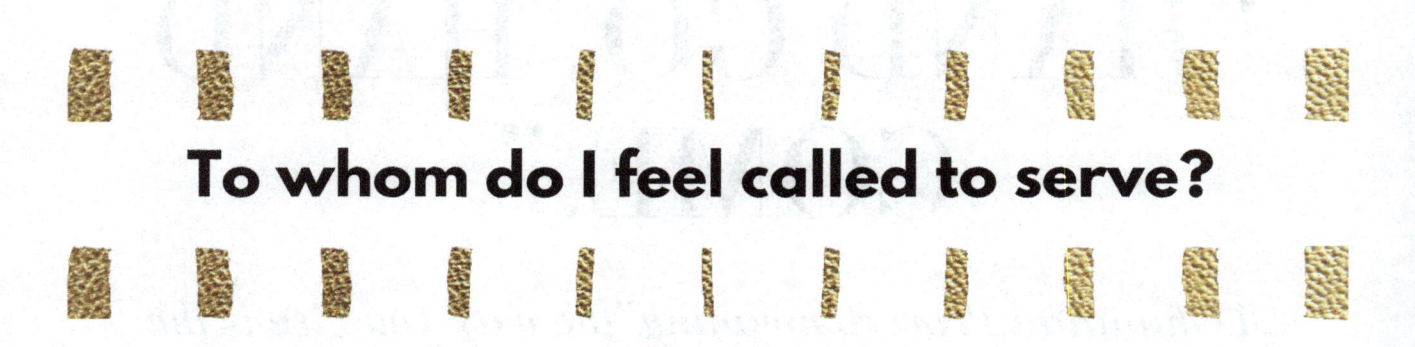

## To whom do I feel called to serve?

"THE PROBLEM THAT BREAKS YOUR HEART IS WHERE YOU ARE MEANT TO SERVE."

*An elder's wisdom.*

Restore integrity in a place you previously caused harm.

With the guidance of an ancestor and trusted elder/wise person, feel into avenues that will allow you to perform an act of atonement or redress for a harm you placed into the world.

Be mindful if reaching out to the person(s) will create more harm. If so, consider how can you perform an act of restitution in another space.

As you perform it, acknowledge the harm you caused and express your intention to reduce the impact of that harm.

Once finished, write about your experience.

# ALL OF US CAN BE FREE.

Color the affirmation.

**What social issues are you unable to ignore or look away from? How might you use your magic and alchemy to actively call forth good in the world?**

# Ritual

[ intention + ceremony ]

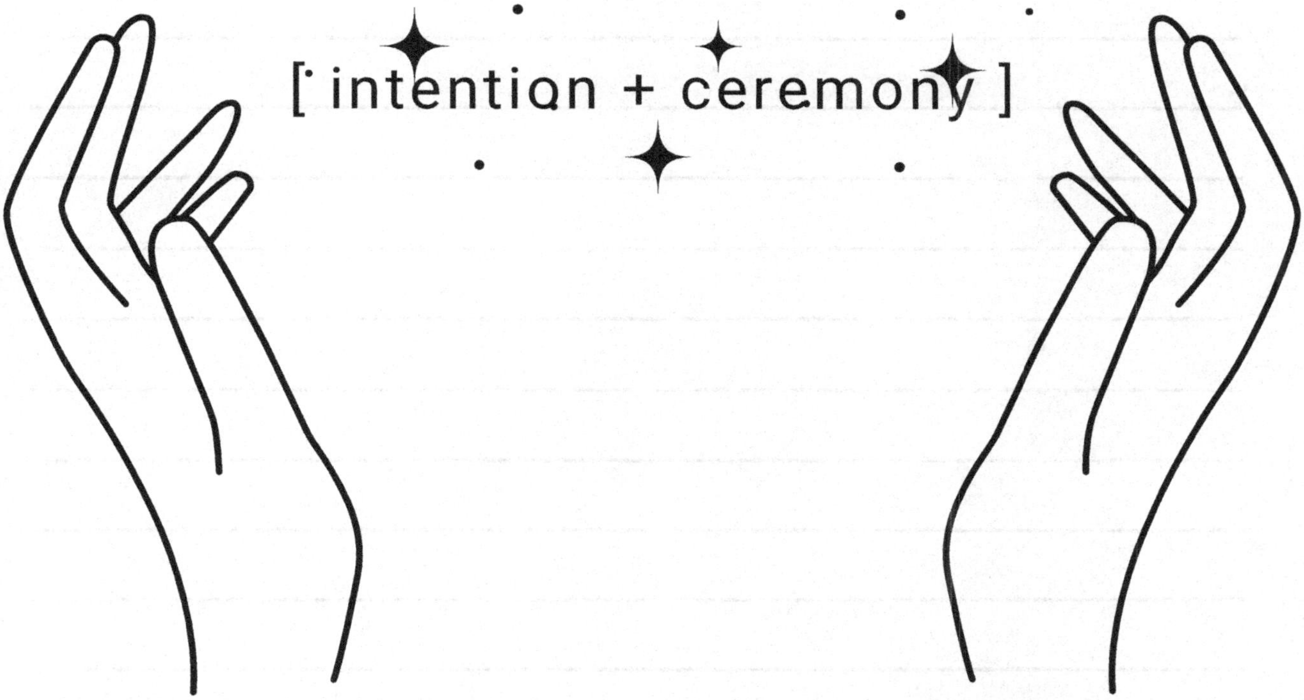

Gather with aligned community around a common intention of collective good.

Decide together what elements you will incorporate and what helpful and loving spirits you will invite into the space.

Ensure each person contributes in a way that aligns with their gifts.

Respond to these next journal prompts in the context of your community and the collective good.

# I am grateful for ...

**What practices or ways of being do you have that cause harm to your family and community?**

**How might you lovingly release them?**

**What support do you need to call forth to help you do so?**

# I am releasing…

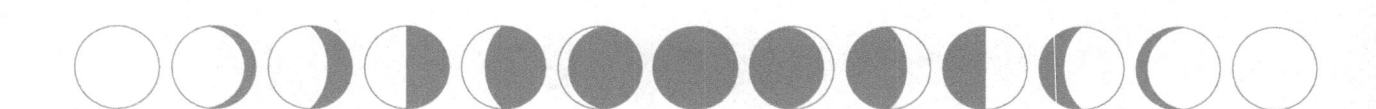

**Do I currently view the earth and natural world as a part of my community?**

**How can I use my connection to the elements to create new ways to care for the earth and the natural world?**

# I am calling forth...

And so it is.
Ase.
Amen.

And so it is.
Ase.
Amen.

# LET US LAUGH IN ALL THE PLACES WE ONCE CRIED.

Color the affirmation.

# Dream

JOURNAL

Use these pages to record your dreams. Pay attention to messages, symbols, and people who appear.

# "BE CAREFUL! I HAD A DREAM..."

*Black Mommas, Grandmommas, and Aunties all across the African Diaspora.*

All across Africa and the Diaspora, it is recognized that dreams are a powerful vehicle for communication and information. An Auntie may have a dream of fish as an omen of an upcoming pregnancy. A great grandmother may dream of numbers to use to play the lottery. A mother may have a dream that acts as a warning about a danger to avoid.

Dreams contain symbolism that offer us messages that we miss in waking life and is a place where the ancestors and other spiritual guides may visit us and offer comfort or guidance. It helps to have a journal near the bed to record our dreams so we don't miss any important messages.

# Miracle

TRACKER

Use these pages to track miracles as they occur. Miracles are happening every day. Atune yourself to miracles of all kinds by strengthening your ability to recognize them.

| JAN | FEB | MAR | APR | MAY | JUN | JUL | AUG | SEP | OCT | NOV | DEC |
|---|---|---|---|---|---|---|---|---|---|---|---|

1 2 3 4 5 6 7 8 9 10 11 12 13 14 15 16 17 18 19 20 21 22 23 24 25 26 27 28 29 30 31

| JAN | FEB | MAR | APR | MAY | JUN | JUL | AUG | SEP | OCT | NOV | DEC |
|---|---|---|---|---|---|---|---|---|---|---|---|

1 2 3 4 5 6 7 8 9 10 11 12 13 14 15 16 17 18 19 20 21 22 23 24 25 26 27 28 29 30 31

| | | | | | | | | | | | |
|---|---|---|---|---|---|---|---|---|---|---|---|
| JAN | FEB | MAR | APR | MAY | JUN | JUL | AUG | SEP | OCT | NOV | DEC |

1 2 3 4 5 6 7 8 9 10 11 12 13 14 15 16 17 18 19 20 21 22 23 24 25 26 27 28 29 30 31

| JAN | FEB | MAR | APR | MAY | JUN | JUL | AUG | SEP | OCT | NOV | DEC |
| --- | --- | --- | --- | --- | --- | --- | --- | --- | --- | --- | --- |

1 2 3 4 5 6 7 8 9 10 11 12 13 14 15 16 17 18 19 20 21 22 23 24 25 26 27 28 29 30 31

| JAN | FEB | MAR | APR | MAY | JUN | JUL | AUG | SEP | OCT | NOV | DEC |
|---|---|---|---|---|---|---|---|---|---|---|---|

1 2 3 4 5 6 7 8 9 10 11 12 13 14 15 16 17 18 19 20 21 22 23 24 25 26 27 28 29 30 31

| JAN | FEB | MAR | APR | MAY | JUN | JUL | AUG | SEP | OCT | NOV | DEC |
|---|---|---|---|---|---|---|---|---|---|---|---|

1 2 3 4 5 6 7 8 9 10 11 12 13 14 15 16 17 18 19 20 21 22 23 24 25 26 27 28 29 30 31

| JAN | FEB | MAR | APR | MAY | JUN | JUL | AUG | SEP | OCT | NOV | DEC |
|---|---|---|---|---|---|---|---|---|---|---|---|

1 2 3 4 5 6 7 8 9 10 11 12 13 14 15 16 17 18 19 20 21 22 23 24 25 26 27 28 29 30 31

| JAN | FEB | MAR | APR | MAY | JUN | JUL | AUG | SEP | OCT | NOV | DEC |
|---|---|---|---|---|---|---|---|---|---|---|---|

1 2 3 4 5 6 7 8 9 10 11 12 13 14 15 16 17 18 19 20 21 22 23 24 25 26 27 28 29 30 31

| JAN | FEB | MAR | APR | MAY | JUN | JUL | AUG | SEP | OCT | NOV | DEC |
|---|---|---|---|---|---|---|---|---|---|---|---|

1 2 3 4 5 6 7 8 9 10 11 12 13 14 15 16 17 18 19 20 21 22 23 24 25 26 27 28 29 30 31

| JAN | FEB | MAR | APR | MAY | JUN | JUL | AUG | SEP | OCT | NOV | DEC |
|---|---|---|---|---|---|---|---|---|---|---|---|

1 2 3 4 5 6 7 8 9 10 11 12 13 14 15 16 17 18 19 20 21 22 23 24 25 26 27 28 29 30 31

| JAN | FEB | MAR | APR | MAY | JUN | JUL | AUG | SEP | OCT | NOV | DEC |
|---|---|---|---|---|---|---|---|---|---|---|---|

1 2 3 4 5 6 7 8 9 10 11 12 13 14 15 16 17 18 19 20 21 22 23 24 25 26 27 28 29 30 31

| JAN | FEB | MAR | APR | MAY | JUN | JUL | AUG | SEP | OCT | NOV | DEC |
|---|---|---|---|---|---|---|---|---|---|---|---|

1 2 3 4 5 6 7 8 9 10 11 12 13 14 15 16 17 18 19 20 21 22 23 24 25 26 27 28 29 30 31

| JAN | FEB | MAR | APR | MAY | JUN | JUL | AUG | SEP | OCT | NOV | DEC |
|---|---|---|---|---|---|---|---|---|---|---|---|

1 2 3 4 5 6 7 8 9 10 11 12 13 14 15 16 17 18 19 20 21 22 23 24 25 26 27 28 29 30 31

| JAN | FEB | MAR | APR | MAY | JUN | JUL | AUG | SEP | OCT | NOV | DEC |
|---|---|---|---|---|---|---|---|---|---|---|---|

1 2 3 4 5 6 7 8 9 10 11 12 13 14 15 16 17 18 19 20 21 22 23 24 25 26 27 28 29 30 31

| JAN | FEB | MAR | APR | MAY | JUN | JUL | AUG | SEP | OCT | NOV | DEC |
|---|---|---|---|---|---|---|---|---|---|---|---|

1 2 3 4 5 6 7 8 9 10 11 12 13 14 15 16 17 18 19 20 21 22 23 24 25 26 27 28 29 30 31

| JAN | FEB | MAR | APR | MAY | JUN | JUL | AUG | SEP | OCT | NOV | DEC |
|---|---|---|---|---|---|---|---|---|---|---|---|

1 2 3 4 5 6 7 8 9 10 11 12 13 14 15 16 17 18 19 20 21 22 23 24 25 26 27 28 29 30 31

| JAN | FEB | MAR | APR | MAY | JUN | JUL | AUG | SEP | OCT | NOV | DEC |
|---|---|---|---|---|---|---|---|---|---|---|---|

1 2 3 4 5 6 7 8 9 10 11 12 13 14 15 16 17 18 19 20 21 22 23 24 25 26 27 28 29 30 31

| JAN | FEB | MAR | APR | MAY | JUN | JUL | AUG | SEP | OCT | NOV | DEC |
|---|---|---|---|---|---|---|---|---|---|---|---|

1 2 3 4 5 6 7 8 9 10 11 12 13 14 15 16 17 18 19 20 21 22 23 24 25 26 27 28 29 30 31

| JAN | FEB | MAR | APR | MAY | JUN | JUL | AUG | SEP | OCT | NOV | DEC |
|---|---|---|---|---|---|---|---|---|---|---|---|

1 2 3 4 5 6 7 8 9 10 11 12 13 14 15 16 17 18 19 20 21 22 23 24 25 26 27 28 29 30 31

| JAN | FEB | MAR | APR | MAY | JUN | JUL | AUG | SEP | OCT | NOV | DEC |
|---|---|---|---|---|---|---|---|---|---|---|---|

1 2 3 4 5 6 7 8 9 10 11 12 13 14 15 16 17 18 19 20 21 22 23 24 25 26 27 28 29 30 31

| JAN | FEB | MAR | APR | MAY | JUN | JUL | AUG | SEP | OCT | NOV | DEC |
|---|---|---|---|---|---|---|---|---|---|---|---|

1 2 3 4 5 6 7 8 9 10 11 12 13 14 15 16 17 18 19 20 21 22 23 24 25 26 27 28 29 30 31

# About the Author

Candice D'Meza (B.A. Black Studies; MPA) is an African American-Haitian Mother of three, Multidisciplinary Artist, and Spiritist whose artistic body of work spans across theater performance, playwrighting, multiple literary genres, activism, dance, critical pedagogy, ritual, social practice, documentary, experimental and short film. She uses the textures of grief, the world building of science fiction, afrofuturism, and fantasy, with the spiritual technologies of African and Diasporic African cosmologies to fashion multidisciplinary experiences based in these core values: time is non-linear and fluid; liberation is ever-present and imminent; The Black Imagination is a site of marronage; ancestral veneration and ritual are time travel vehicles that aid us in orienting our personal and collective timelines towards freedom.

Collectively, her work has been featured, grant funded, commissioned, published, screened and archived at institutions across the nation. These include: The Contemporary Art Museum of Houston, DiverseWorks, PlayBill, Latinx Playwrights Circle, BOLD Ventures Grant through the Helen Gurley Foundation, Rice University, Colgate University, The Catastrophic Theatre, The Alley Theatre, The Ensemble Theater, Stages Theater, Houston Arts Alliance, Red Bull Arts, The City of Houston, Black Spatial Relics, American Theatre Magazine, The Acentos Review, Houston Press, the Houston Chronicle, and various national film festivals. She is a proud member of the Actors Equity Union and a four time award winner at the Houston Press Theater Awards, including the 2018 win for Best Utility Player.

To learn more about her and her work, visit her website at www.candicedmeza.com

Made in the USA
Las Vegas, NV
20 December 2023

83277446R00138